THIS CHANGES EVERYTHING

2 CORINTHIANS 5:17

Published by: YM360

NAME

DATE

THIS
CHANGES
EVERYTHING
—
2 CORINTHIANS 5:17

TABLE OF
CONTENTS

THIS CHANGES EVERYTHING

The world looks a certain way. The status quo. It is what it is. Things will never change.

Until it does.

Something happens. Something big. A complete 180° turn from death to life.

That something is Jesus Christ.

The power of the Gospel is transformative. It takes hearts of stone and turns them into hearts of flesh. It flips the light switch on darkness. It resurrects the dead and breathes life into them. It delivers hope, it offers peace, and it changes everything.

If you're ready to come into contact with the love and grace of Jesus Christ, if you're ready for nothing in your life to be the same, then it's time to jump into This Changes Everything. Let's go.

HAVE YOU PREPARED FOR THE JOURNEY?

Ask yourself: Is my heart prepared to be challenged? Am I willing to be changed? If you can't answer "yes" to these questions, this journey might not be nearly as spectacular as it could be. If you need to, take a moment and silently talk to God in prayer. Ask God to radically move in your life.

YOU'RE HOLDING YOUR MAP

This book your holding is the road map for your journey. It will help guide your experiences. Write your name and date in the front. Hold on to it. You may want to look back and remember this time in your life.

LEARN. AND TEACH.

Keep your eyes and ears open for those valuable moments where God wants to teach you something. But don't miss the chance to teach your friends and be taught by them. Your friends are with you in this experience. Be open to what God is doing in and through them, and how He might be using them to speak to you. And vice versa.

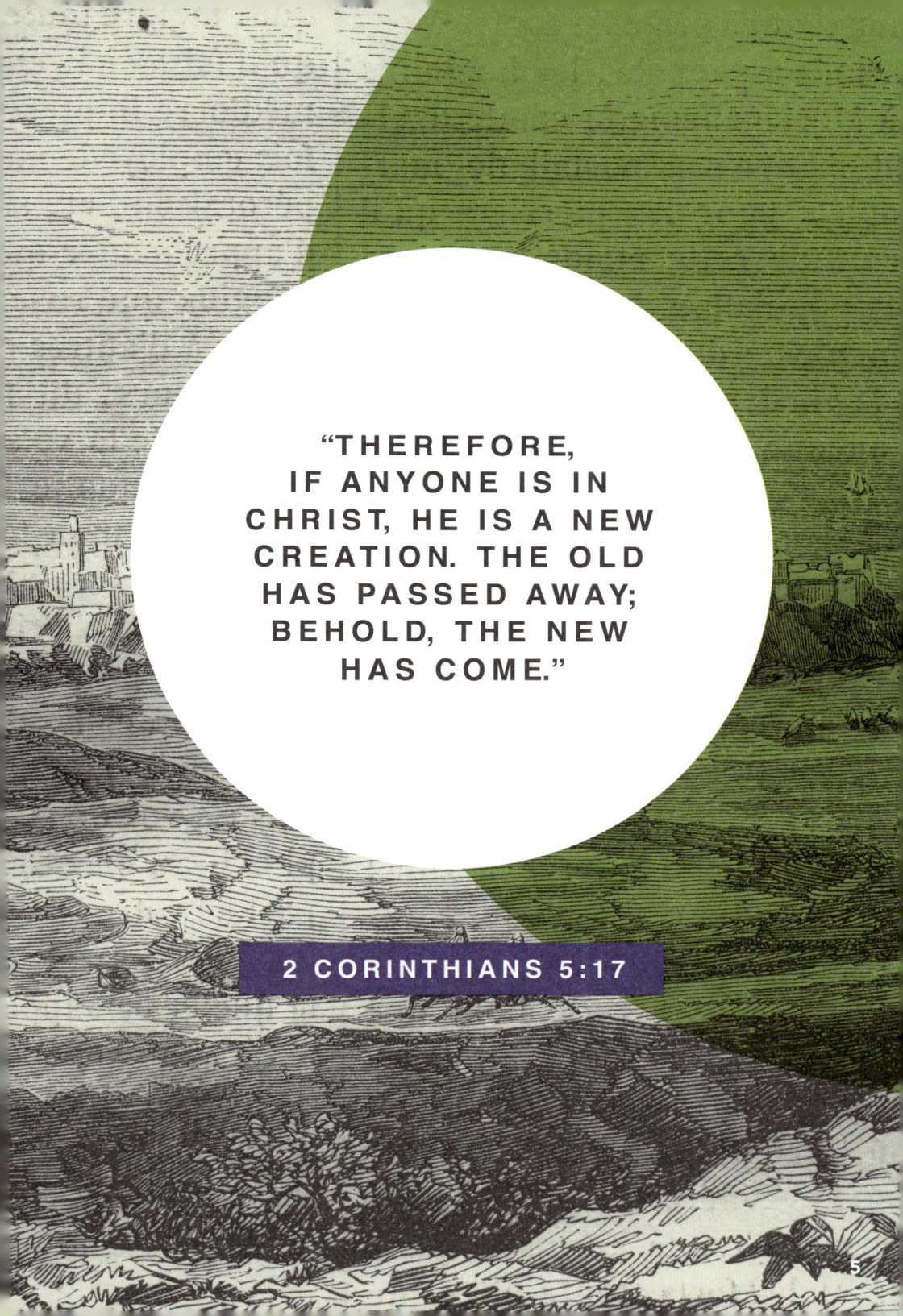

"THEREFORE, IF ANYONE IS IN CHRIST, HE IS A NEW CREATION. THE OLD HAS PASSED AWAY; BEHOLD, THE NEW HAS COME."

2 CORINTHIANS 5:17

LARGE GROUP

NOTES

SESSION 1

These pages are designed for any notes you might want to jot down during this Large Group session. There's a lot of awesome stuff you're going to be learning. So, even if you're not much of a note taker, you might want to at least jot down what you think is important.

TRY WRITING DOWN:
- Any specific teaching points
- Verse references for Scripture passages
- Quotes that make you think
- Anything you have a question about

Origin stories. They're important because they give context.

Take superheroes for instance. They have the best origin stories because, often, they clue you in to what makes them the way they are. Once you know that Dex-Starr was an abandoned kitten who was almost drowned by hoodlums, you totally get why he would seek vengeance on street kids.

When we get the backstory on someone, it becomes easier to understand what drives them in the present day. And just like superheroes (or super cat villains), we each have an origin story. And so does humanity.

In this first Small Group, we're going to look into the origin story of us as people. We're going to learn how we got here. And we're going to take a peek at where we're headed.

Ready? Let's jump in.

ORIGIN STORIES

For each of the superheroes listed in the column on the left, match their origin story from the column on the right.

SUPERHEROS & SUPERVILLANS

Batman

Superman

Nightman

The Whizzer

Catwoman

Squirrel Girl

Dex-Starr

SUPERHEROS & SUPERVILLANS

An abandoned kitten nearly drowned by hoodlums is transformed into an evil villain by the power of his rage.

A flight attendant who is struck on the head during a plane crash and left with amnesia whose father owned a pet store.

A saxophone-playing jazz singer gets struck by lightning on a cable car, giving him super-powers, but making it difficult for him to sleep.

A young girl grew a tail.

A rich man stands up to his fear of flying mammals and becomes one.

A young man was bitten by a cobra, so his father injected him with mongoose blood, giving him super-speed.

An alien that was sent to earth and must hide in plain sight.

MY ORIGIN STORY

Work through the following activities with your group to unpack what they mean for your life.

PROMPT 1:
Describe in a few sentences how your life was growing up.

PROMPT 2:
Describe who was primarily responsible for raising you.

PROMPT 3:
Describe a few of the main blessings that have defined your life.

PROMPT 4:
Describe some of the struggles that have defined your life.

PROMPT 5:
If you had to imagine, write down a few sentences on where you think your life is headed.

"But now, the righteousness of God has been manifested apart from the law, although the Law and the Prophets bear witness to it — the righteousness of God through faith in Jesus Christ for all who believe. For there is no distinction: for all have sinned and fallen short of the glory of God..." - Romans 3:21-23

• What is Romans 3:21-23 saying?

• Do you agree with this passage in Scripture? Why or why not?

• If all have sinned and fallen short of the glory of God, what does that mean in our relationship with Him?

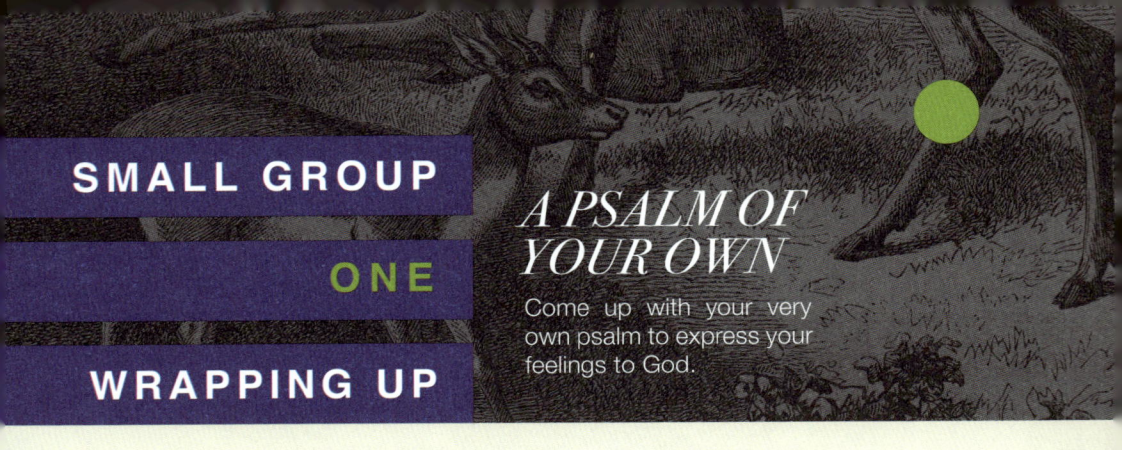

A PSALM OF YOUR OWN

Come up with your very own psalm to express your feelings to God.

PROMPT 1:
What do you say in your heart about God? Don't hold back. Be honest.

PROMPT 2:
If God were to look down from heaven on you, what would He see within your heart?

PROMPT 3:
If your sin were an outward manifestation on you physically, what would you look like?

PROMPT 4:
In verse 7, the psalmist talks about the salvation coming for Israel. How do you visualize salvation coming for you?

Now build a psalm similar to the one you read in Psalm 14:1-7. Be creative!

"FOR ALL HAVE SINNED AND FALL SHORT OF THE GLORY OF GOD, AND ARE JUSTIFIED BY HIS GRACE AS A GIFT, THROUGH THE REDEMPTION THAT IS IN CHRIST JESUS."

ROMANS 3:23-24

These pages are designed for any notes you might want to jot down during this Large Group session. There's a lot of awesome stuff you're going to be learning. So, even if you're not much of a note taker, you might want to at least jot down what you think is important.

TRY WRITING DOWN:
- Any specific teaching points
- Verse references for Scripture passages
- Quotes that make you think
- Anything you have a question about

SMALL GROUP

TWO

INTRO

Has there ever been a moment in your life where everything changed? Maybe it was a big change. Like the birth of a sibling. Or moving to a new city. Maybe it was a small change. Maybe you switched positions on your team. Or maybe you got a new haircut. Regardless, these moments mark the end of the way something was and the beginning of the way things are from then on.

Change can sometimes be scary. But it can also be awesome.

When it comes to God's plan for humankind, there was always a big change in the works. The plan started with God's love for us. And because He loved us so much, He planned on fighting for us. He planned on making a way for us to know a new life of purpose and meaning and . . . life.

This new change made it possible for you to experience a truth about your life that you could never have imagined otherwise.

In Small Group 2, you'll discover what this change is and how, once you experience it, you'll never be the same again.

THE MOMENT IT ALL CHANGED

Read the following scenarios. Then see who can be the most creative in making up the way the story ends.

SCENARIO #1

You're at the library studying when you see the person you have a huge crush on. They come over to talk to you. Everything changes when they suddenly open their mouth and you notice they have a huge piece of broccoli in their teeth. What happens next?

SCENARIO #2

You post a picture on Instagram of yourself looking your best. Your friends all seem to love it. But everything changes when your mom leaves a comment telling you she's going by the store and asks if you need her to pick you up some more acne cream. What happens next?

SCENARIO #3

You're giving a speech in front of your Social Studies class and you're rocking it, until you notice a few people laughing. Everything changes when you realize your zipper is undone! What happens next?

SCENARIO #4

You're walking through the lunch room carrying a huge tray full of food. Everything changes when you turn a corner and dump your entire tray on the most popular girl in school. What happens next?

SCENARIO #5

You're browsing Instagram checking out what's going on with the world. Everything changes when you see your sibling has uploaded the video (you thought he/she had already deleted) of you singing your favorite song in your bathrobe. What happens next?

HOW IT ALL CHANGED

Work with your group to discuss how Jesus changed everything.

GOD ⟵——————⟶ **PEOPLE**

- What is sin?

- What are the consequences of sin?

- Why are there consequences?

Before we look to the Bible to see how Jesus changed everything, we need to define three words. How would you define the following words?

REDEEM

FORGIVE

UNITE

READ EPHESIANS 1:7-10.

> "7 In him we have redemption through his blood, the forgiveness of our trespasses, according to the riches of his grace, 8 which he lavished upon us, in all wisdom and insight 9 making known to us the mystery of his will, according to his purpose, which he set forth in Christ 10 as a plan for the fullness of time, to unite all things in him, things in heaven and things on earth."

• Look at verse 7. You just defined the word "redeem." Why did we need redeeming?

• What did Jesus redeem us from?

• How did He do it?

• Verses 8-10 tell us that this was God's plan all along. What does verse 10 tell us is the purpose of God's plan to redeem us through Jesus' sacrifice?

NOW, READ GALATIANS 4:4-7.

> "4 But when the fullness of time had come, God sent forth his Son, born of woman, born under the law, 5 to redeem those who were under the law, so that we might receive adoption as sons. 6 And because you are sons, God has sent the Spirit of his Son into our hearts, crying, 'Abba! Father!' 7 So you are no longer a slave, but a son, and if a son, then an heir through God."

• Verse 5 tells us of another purpose of God's plan to redeem us. What is it?

• What does this say about God's great love for you?

• How does the fact that you can been adopted as a child of God change the way you see Jesus, and your faith in general?

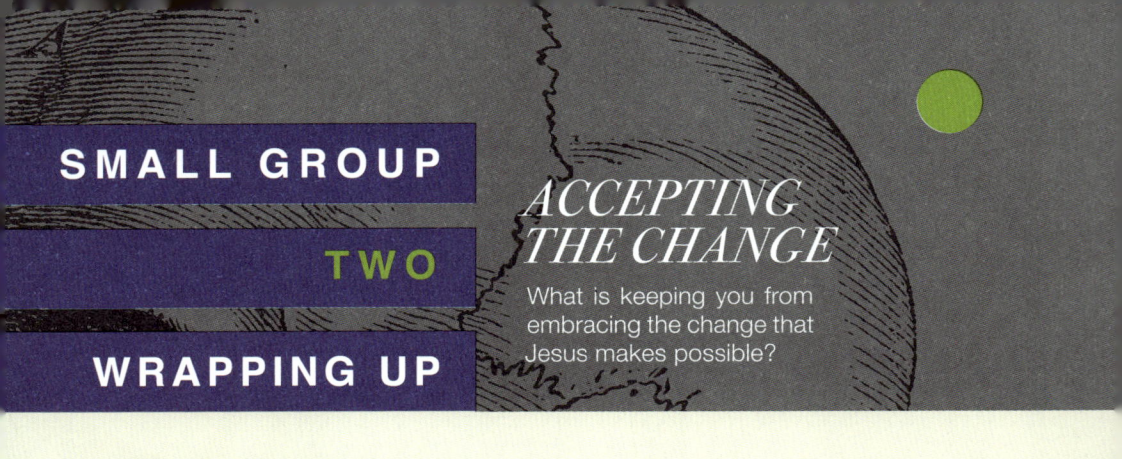

ACCEPTING THE CHANGE

What is keeping you from embracing the change that Jesus makes possible?

READ ROMANS 10:9-13

"9 If you confess with your mouth that Jesus is Lord and believe in your heart that God raised him from the dead, you will be saved. 10 For with the heart one believes and is justified, and with the mouth one confesses and is saved. 11 For the Scripture says, 'Everyone who believes in him will not be put to shame.' 12 For there is no distinction between Jew and Greek; for the same Lord is Lord of all, bestowing his riches on all who call on him. 13 For 'everyone who calls on the name of the Lord will be saved.'"

• If you have been adopted by God into His family, what do you have to say to Him in response?

• If you have yet to be adopted into God's family, and still aren't ready to accept the radical change He offers, what is keeping you from accepting the redemption Jesus has purchased for you?

• If you have never accepted the redemption offered through faith in Christ, and are wanting to be adopted into God's family, express this desire to God now. Then, let an adult in your group know of your decision.

"IF YOU CONFESS WITH YOUR MOUTH THAT JESUS IS LORD AND BELIEVE IN YOUR HEART THAT GOD RAISED HIM FROM THE DEAD, YOU WILL BE SAVED. FOR WITH THE HEART ONE BELIEVES AND IS JUSTIFIED, AND WITH THE MOUTH ONE CONFESSES AND IS SAVED."

ROMANS 10:9-10

These pages are designed for any notes you might want to jot down during this Large Group session. There's a lot of awesome stuff you're going to be learning. So, even if you're not much of a note taker, you might want to at least jot down what you think is important.

TRY WRITING DOWN:
- Any specific teaching points
- Verse references for Scripture passages
- Quotes that make you think
- Anything you have a question about

SMALL GROUP

THREE

INTRO

When you're a believer in Christ, your life looks different from the rest of the world. The things that are important to the world (things like status, power, and wealth) aren't necessarily your focus.

Scripture gives us a very clear picture of how our lives should look when they have been transformed by Jesus. This new existence is defined by knowing Christ (who He is, what He's about, and what He asks of us), and making Him known to everyone around us. We get a spotlight on our priorities and our faith that is expressed through our purpose and life.

Does your life look this way? Has your normal, everyday existence been radically changed by the Gospel?

Let's jump in and look at what's important to believers and how to live like a Christ-follower who has been fundamentally changed.

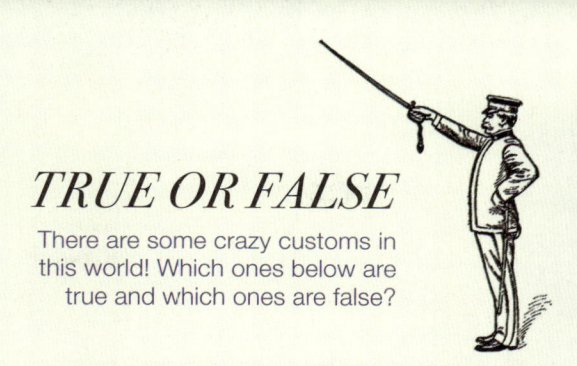

TRUE OR FALSE

There are some crazy customs in this world! Which ones below are true and which ones are false?

SCENARIO #1
It's rude to smell food in Tanzania.

SCENARIO #2
In Thailand, you only use your fork to push your food onto your spoon, never to eat with.

SCENARIO #3
In all places in the world, it's considered offensive to sit in the front seat of a cab.

SCENARIO #4
The Nigerian Kogoro tribe prohibits their women from using spoons, so don't ever ask a woman for one.

SCENARIO #5
Always stick your chopsticks in your rice when you're taking a rest during a meal in Japan.

WHAT'S THE DEAL?

Work with your group to discover how the Gospel impacts your life today.

"12 Put on then, as God's chosen ones, holy and beloved, compassionate hearts, kindness, humility, meekness, and patience, 13 bearing with one another and, if one has a complaint against another, forgiving each other; as the Lord has forgiven you, so you also must forgive. 14 And above all these put on love, which binds everything together in perfect harmony. 15 And let the peace of Christ rule in your hearts, to which indeed you were called in one body. And be thankful." - Colossians 3:12–15

- Who are God's chosen ones, holy and beloved?

- What do you think it means to have a compassionate heart?

- What do you think it means to be kind?

- What is the difference between humility, meekness, and patience?

- What do you think it means to bear with one another?

- What other points jump out in this text for you?

TRIALS AND TRIBULATIONS

Think of a situation that you or someone you are close to has been through a difficult time. Write down the event that happened. How did you or they react? Why did that stick with you?

NOW ANSWER THE FOLLOWING QUESTIONS:

• Remember James says to count it as "joy." What do you think joy means?

• Is joy different than happiness?

• Why do you think it's important for believers to know the difference between joy and happiness?

• How will this new definition of "counting it joy" change the way you encounter hardship?

A NEW HEART AND ABUNDANT LIFE

Answer the questions below. You don't have to share them if you don't want to, so be open and honest with yourself.

• How has (or how could) God changed you inwardly?

• How have you expressed that outwardly?

• How might God give your future trials and hardships in life new purpose with Him?

"Imagine yourself as a living house. God comes in to rebuild that house. At first, perhaps, you can understand what He is doing. He is getting the drains right and stopping the leaks in the roof and so on; you knew that those jobs needed doing and so you are not surprised. But presently He starts knocking the house about in a way that hurts abominably and does not seem to make any sense. What on earth is He up to? The explanation is that He is building quite a different house from the one you thought of - throwing out a new wing here, putting on an extra floor there, running up towers, making courtyards. You thought you were being made into a decent little cottage: but He is building a palace. He intends to come and live in it Himself."

C.S. LEWIS

Take some time to write out a prayer, engaging with Him as He asks to come inside and transform your heart (or continue the work He's already begun).

"AND ABOVE ALL THESE PUT ON LOVE, WHICH BINDS EVERYTHING TOGETHER IN PERFECT HARMONY."

COLOSSIANS 3:14

LARGE GROUP
NOTES

SESSION 4

These pages are designed for any notes you might want to jot down during this Large Group session. There's a lot of awesome stuff you're going to be learning. So, even if you're not much of a note taker, you might want to at least jot down what you think is important.

TRY WRITING DOWN:
- Any specific teaching points
- Verse references for Scripture passages
- Quotes that make you think
- Anything you have a question about

SMALL GROUP
FOUR
INTRO

There is nothing quite like the anticipation that comes with waiting for something really awesome. Whether you're waiting for a new phone, an upcoming event with friends, a family vacation, or anything similar, the emotions you experience in the waiting are part of the fun.

But the other side of the coin is when you're waiting for something unpleasant to be over. Maybe you have a teacher who is not very nice and you're waiting for the semester to be over. Maybe you just broke up with a boyfriend or girlfriend and you're waiting to get over them. Maybe your parents are going through a divorce. Maybe you have a relative who is sick. Sometimes, waiting can be pretty rough.

When we look at our lives, it's so easy to feel overwhelmed. Sure there are times when we wait for really fun things. But there are times when we wait through tough things that can leave us depressed and down. And yet, God has promised that one day He will make all things new. We can trust His word. We can actively live as children of this promise, all the while hoping in a future where everything will be made right and we are fully redeemed.

That is what this session is about. Let's dive in.

WAIT FOR IT!

When is the wait worth it? Work with your group to complete the following activity.

CAN YOU NAME A TIME WHEN YOU FOUND YOURSELF LOOKING FORWARD TO SOMETHING REALLY AWESOME?

HOW LONG DID YOU HAVE TO WAIT?

WHAT DID IT FEEL LIKE WHILE YOU HAD TO WAIT?

WHAT EMOTIONS DID YOU FEEL WHEN YOU FINALLY GOT TO EXPERIENCE THE THING YOU WERE WAITING ON?

FINAL QUESTION: WAS IT WORTH THE WAIT?

HOLDING ON FOR THE FUTURE

Work through the following passages with your group to learn about how the Gospel will one day TRULY change everything.

"16 So we do not lose heart. Though our outer self is wasting away, our inner self is being renewed day by day. 17 For this light momentary affliction is preparing for us an eternal weight of glory beyond all comparison, 18 as we look not to the things that are seen but to the things that are unseen. For the things that are seen are transient, but the things that are unseen are eternal." - 2 Corinthians 4:16–18.

Paul makes a number of contrasts here. Can you name them all?

Outer self   vs.

Wasting away   vs.

Light   vs.

Momentary   vs.

Affliction   vs.

What we can see vs.

• Now, look at vs. 16. When Paul says we don't lose heart, he is talking about being bold. Can you guess what Paul is encouraging us to be bold about?

• What do you think Paul means when he says, "our outer self is wasting away"?

• What does Paul say happens to our inner self? Does anyone have any idea what Paul may be talking about here?

• Whoa! How does Paul describe his troubles in vs. 17? Knowing what you just read in 2 Corinthians 11, would you describe them as "light"? What words would you use to describe them?

• Here's another contrast: "Light and momentary affliction" versus an "eternal weight of glory" so good it can't be described. What exactly is Paul saying?

• In verse 18, Paul helps us know how to process the hard times we experience because we're Christ-followers. He does it with another contrast. What is he contrasting, and how does this help us deal with the tough times we face?

READ REVELATION 22:1-5 AS A GROUP TO SEE WHAT GOD IS DOING TO CHANGE EVERYTHING.

"1Then the angel showed me the river of the water of life, bright as crystal, flowing from the throne of God and of the Lamb 2 through the middle of the street of the city; also, on either side of the river, the tree of life with its twelve kinds of fruit, yielding its fruit each month. The leaves of the tree were for the healing of the nations. 3 No longer will there be anything accursed, but the throne of God and of the Lamb will be in it, and his servants will worship him. 4 They will see his face, and his name will be on their foreheads. 5 And night will be no more. They will need no light of lamp or sun, for the Lord God will be their light, and they will reign forever and ever." - Revelation 22:1–5.

Take a moment and circle every place in the passage that speaks to a new future where God has redeemed the world from the consequences of sin.

• The first hint we have of God redeeming a broken world is in verse 2. What were the leaves of the tree of life for?

• In the world around you every day, what are some examples of the kind of conflict you see between people?

• What are some examples of the conflict we see between countries and nations?

• Look at verse 3. When John talks about the "accursed," he is talking about the consequences of sin. He says here that there will be no consequences of sin anymore. What are some of the consequences of sin?

• Look at verse 4. What will be our relationship with God?

• What does verse 5 tell us about the future of this new reality?

KNOWING THE FUTURE THAT GOD IS PLANNING GIVES US HOPE. AND HOPE MAKES US BOLD.

THE FUTURE GOD IS PLANNING COULD HAPPEN AT ANY MOMENT. IT COULD HAPPEN RIGHT NOW. HOW DOES THAT CHANGE THE WAY YOU THINK ABOUT LIVING YOUR LIFE FOR CHRIST?

CAN YOU THINK OF THREE TO FIVE WAYS IN WHICH YOU COULD BE BOLDER IN LIVING OUT YOUR FAITH?

WHAT ABOUT YOUR ATTITUDE? DO YOU GET HOPELESS AT TIMES? HOW CAN KNOWING WHAT GOD IS PLANNING IN THE FUTURE IMPACT YOUR PRESENT?

CLOSING

If there's one thing we know about the Gospel, it's that it demands a reaction. Once you hear the story of Jesus leaving heaven and coming to earth to redeem us, you have to respond.

Over the course of the last four sessions, you and your friends have walked through the story of the Gospel: from the fall of man, to Christ's death and resurrection. You've seen how believers are called to live. You've seen how we have a hope that is greater than any temporary hope this world has to offer.

No matter what, now that you've experienced these last four session, you KNOW. You've encountered the Good News and there's a choice set before you.

Maybe you came into this event already in a relationship with the Lord. It's possible that you renewed that commitment, or asked God to help you re-tune your heart to Him. Maybe you walk closely with the Lord already, and this was just a sweet time to grow in Him and in your community.

Of course, there's always the option of apathy. Maybe you came to this event because a parent made you, or your crush was here. Maybe you just came because that's what you've always done. And when the choice was set before you: life or death, it's not that you chose death, it's that you didn't choose life. You can ignore the question, but that, in and of itself, is an answer.

But it's very possible that something changed within you during this event. That the Holy Spirit revealed to you that Jesus loves you, died for you, and deeply wants to have a relationship with you. That your life is more than just about who you date, what sports you play, or where you live. Your life can be about the gospel. It can be used to bring glory to God.

If you're still on the fence, keep praying. If you don't know what next steps to take, ask someone. If you're confused, keep seeking. Look for the ways God is calling you out of your normal life, and into change that transforms all of it.

DEVOTION ONE

This is the first of four *This Changes Everything* devotions. Find some time to work through them during your study of *This Changes Everything*.

WHEN EVERYTHING CHANGED for Mary, Mother of Jesus

SIMPLE TRUTH: The Gospel not only changes our eternal future, it changes our day-to-day lives as well.

FIRST, read Luke 1:26-38, then answer the following questions:

- Look at verse 29. Why do you think Mary reacted the way she did? Visualize the situation that is being described in these verses. Put yourself in her shoes. How would you react?

- Summarize the angel's announcement to Mary in verses 30-33.

- Mary's main concern was a practical one (she wondered how she would have a baby because she had never had sexual relations with a man). How did the angel respond when she shared what was on her mind?

- There is an amazing promise in verse 37. What is it?

- Sum up Mary's response in verse 38.

NOW, read this:

You've been talking about the power of the Gospel to change things. To change people's future. To change the world. To change people's purpose. In the story you just read today, we get the chance to see one of the best examples of how the Gospel changed one person's life in such an amazing way it's kind of hard to even fathom.

You do realize that Mary was almost certainly a teenager, right? Most scholars think she was

14-years-old or so. Is it possible to imagine even a little bit of what it must have felt like to have been Mary? I mean, an angel appears to you (which, even if he hadn't said a word would have been unbelievably amazing) and tells you that you are the woman God has chosen to use to bring His only Son into this world. You want to talk about the Gospel changing everything?!?!

The Greek word we translate to get the word gospel literally means "the good news." The angel's good news changed Mary's life forever, in ways that we can barely begin to understand. What must it have been like to be the earthly mother of God's Son? What must it have been like to watch Him grow up, knowing He was special but not having a clue about what His life would ultimately look like? What must it have been like to watch your son begin His ministry? Can you imagine looking on the cross and seeing your boy – your firstborn and God's only – die the cruelest death? The Gospel very literally changed everything for Mary.

Here's the coolest part: Jesus didn't just change Mary's day-to-day life in the way a child changes every mother's life. He changed her eternity. Mary was Jesus' mother. But He was her Savior. The faith Mary had in the person and work of Jesus saved her in the same manner that faith saves everyone. The Gospel changed everything for Mary. Everything.

FINALLY, consider this:

1. The Gospel changed Mary's day-to-day life in a unique way. How has the Gospel changed your day-to-day life?

2. The Gospel changed Mary's future, as well. In two or three sentences, describe how the Gospel impacts your future.

3. God used Mary in a way that He hasn't used anyone since. God may not use you in ways that are as miraculous (though He certainly could if He chose to), but God has a plan for you. God wants to work in and through you to change the world for His sake. Spend a few moments in prayer today telling God that, like Mary, you stand ready to follow where He leads.

DEVOTION TWO

WHEN EVERYTHING CHANGED for Mary Magdalene

SIMPLE TRUTH: Mary Magdalene's life was changed forever when she encountered Jesus.

We don't have a lot of stories about Mary Magdalene in scripture, but with a little bit of detective work, we can learn about this woman who loved Jesus and how her life was changed by Him.

FIRST, read Luke 8:1-3 and Mark 16:9, then answer the following questions:

- What do these short scriptures tell us about Mary Magdalene?

- Who healed Mary Magdalene of her "seven demons"?

- What did Mary Magdalene do with her life after Jesus healed her?

- Why do you think that event changed everything for Mary Magdalene?

NOW, read this:

Mary Magdalene was changed by her encounter with Jesus. It doesn't happen in the narrative of the scripture, but Luke and Mark tell us that Jesus healed her from seven demons. We don't necessarily know what that means: maybe a physical or mental illness, or maybe seven actual demons. Whatever it was, after that happened, it appears that Mary (like the disciples), dropped everything in her life and followed Jesus. Luke 8:3 even says that she was part of the group that helped to fund the travels of Jesus and His disciples, which means that she even gave her finances to the cause of Christ. Matthew 27:56, Mark 15:40, and John 19:25 all mention Mary Magdalene being at Jesus's crucifixion, and Mark 16:1 states she was in the group of women who went to Jesus's tomb to anoint His body. Which means she was a part of the group who first saw Jesus resurrected.

Loyal to the end (anointing the body of a recently executed criminal probably wasn't the safest bet she could have made), faithful in the midst of grief (the women came to tend to His body when the rest of the disciples were in hiding), Mary Magdalene's short narrative throughout the Gospels is a great reminder to us that the transformation that God stirs in us can survive even our most difficult moments. And that we give what we have where we can. Mary used every resource she had at her disposal for the advancement of Jesus's message. She stuck with Him, even when fear and doubt surely set in.

FINALLY, consider this:

1. Have you experienced fears or doubts about Jesus or your relationship with Him?

2. What actions on the part of Mary Magdalene played a role in her fearlessness when it came to following Jesus?

3. In what way has Jesus changed your life that would cause you to live like Mary Magdalene?

DEVOTION THREE

This is the third of four *This Changes Everything* devotions. Find some time to work through them during your study of *This Changes Everything*.

WHEN EVERYTHING CHANGED for the Disciples

SIMPLE TRUTH: Through the Gospel, God gives a new purpose and mission.

FIRST, read Matthew 4:18-22, then answer the following questions:

• What did Jesus say exactly to Peter and Andrew?

• What stands out to you about what He said?

• How did Peter and Andrew, and then later, James and John, respond?

• What jumps out to you as important about how they responded?

• The word "immediately" is an adverb. If you remember your grammar, an adverb is a word that describes or "modifies" another word or phrase. In this case "immediately" describes the manner in which the disciples left their boats and nets. Why is this important? How else might they have responded?

NOW, read this:
It's so easy to read the story of Jesus calling His first disciples and breeze right past the HUGE implications this story has. Not only does this story contain a pretty major personal impact on the lives of the individual disciples, it has significant ramifications for the world as we know it. Seriously. The working of the Gospel as we see it in this story has MAJOR

potential. Let's unpack it a bit.

When Jesus called these specific disciples, He wasn't just calling "average Joe's" to follow Him. Well, that's not exactly true. At the moment Jesus called Peter, Andrew, James, and John, they were the most average of Joe's. But what Jesus knew is that, through the power of the Gospel, they would be transformed into some of the most influential leaders of the movement of Christianity.

Peter would become the leader of the disciples and one of the most important figures of the early Church. John would be known as the "beloved disciple," and would write the Gospel of John, along with 1, 2, and 3rd John, and Revelation. Along the way, they would be a main part of the rapid and powerful spread of the Gospel throughout the world, the power of which is still being felt all around the world even as you read this. All that because they answered Jesus' call to follow Him.

Don't miss what Jesus did for these men. Jesus changed their purpose. Their vocation, their jobs, was "fishermen." They spent every day fishing. This was their purpose. Their job. The task that defined them. Jesus changed that with two words: "follow me." Soon, these men came to saving faith in Jesus, and the Gospel working in and through them changed their lives. The same is true with you. The Gospel gives you a new purpose and a new meaning. You simply have to embrace it. What are you waiting on?

FINALLY, consider this:

1. What about your life's purpose has the Gospel changed?

2. How has the Gospel given your life new and deeper meaning?

3. Would you describe yourself as simply a believer in Jesus? Or are you a follower of Jesus? What is keeping you from "leaving your nets" and following Jesus with your whole life?

DEVOTION FOUR

WHEN EVERYTHING CHANGED for the Ethiopian Court Official

SIMPLE TRUTH: The Ethiopian Court Official's life was changed when Phillip heeded the call to tell him about Jesus.

We first meet Phillip in Acts 6:5, where we learn he's a part of a kind of first wave of believers in Christ. Phillip is sometimes called Phillip the Evangelist, because of his role in spreading the Gospel in the early days of the church.

FIRST, read Act 8:26-40, then answer the following questions:

• How did Phillip know to go out on the road and speak to the Ethiopian?

• What is significant about the passage of scripture the Ethiopian was reading?

• How did the Ethiopian respond to what Phillip told him?

NOW, read this:

As we move through the story of scripture in the New Testament, we get further from people who actually encountered Jesus in the flesh. If the good news was going to spread, it was up to those who experienced Jesus to tell others, and for those others to keep it going. Phillip was one of those who never met Jesus on earth, but his life was so changed by the Gospel that he became one of its biggest cheerleaders. All throughout Acts, we read about this missionary journey or that missionary journey. In this story, he's nudged by the Holy Spirit to go to a certain road, where he finds an official from the court of Candice, queen of the Ethiopians, reading Isaiah. Phillip asks the official if he understands what he's reading, and the man answers "How can I unless someone guides me?" So right then and there, Phillip sits down with him and helps him to unpack the scripture, which just so happens (not really, God planned it) to be a prophesy about Jesus. By the end of the conversation, the Ethiopian is baptized, and he "goes away rejoicing."

There's a lot to unpack here. First, Phillip's quick and all-in "yes" to the Spirit leading him to find the Ethiopian. There are so many times in life when we will feel these urgings from the Holy Spirit to talk to someone or pray for someone. These are easy to ignore because...well, frankly, they are slightly uncomfortable for some people. But let's consider the options of Phillip ignoring the Spirit here. The Ethiopian continues to be confused about the scripture, he doesn't understand what he's reading, and he goes back home, frustrated. What Phillip did when he listened and obeyed was not just about the Ethiopian. A high court official who had a miraculous experience and now knew Jesus was primed to share the gospel in his own land, with the queen, and to his people. He took Jesus back to Ethiopia.

God was able to tell an even bigger story than just a Spirit-led meeting on a road between Jerusalem and Gaza. He used these two men to spread the good news of Jesus to places it could never go on its own. He chose to include them in His story.

He does the same thing with us. He doesn't need us, certainly, but in His graciousness, He allows us to partner with Him.

FINALLY, consider this:

1. Have you ever been scared to follow-through when you've felt the Spirit asking you to step out in faith?

2. How can you learn to listen more closely for opportunities to share Jesus with others as you return from this event?

ANDY BLANKS

Andy is the Co-Founder and Publisher for YM360. Andy lives in Birmingham, AL with his wonderful wife Brendt, their three daughters, and one son. He's a pretty big fan of both the Boston Red Sox and anything involving the Auburn Tigers. When he's not hanging out with his family or volunteering at his church's youth ministry, you can find Andy trail running or mountain biking.

ERIN MOON

Erin is the Creative Director for YM360, and the Co-Worker You Are Least Likely to Want On Your Cornhole Team. Besides being absolutely terrible at cornhole, she adores working at YM360 to help create resources as a way to help teenagers consider the Gospel in fresh ways. A displaced Texan in Alabama, Erin is wife to Ben, momma bear to Holland and Marlo, and an ardent fan of TV binge watching.

LAUREL-DAWN BERRYHILL

Laurel-Dawn is YM360's Art Director. A military kid who bounced around the US before finally landing in Birmingham, LD graduated from Auburn University and began making the world a beautiful place through the graphic arts. In her spare time you can find her painting, honing her emoji game, and investing in the daily coconut-popsicles-and-water-sprinklers ritual with her son, Lochlan.

Other awesome folks who helped make this thing happen:

J. ROGER DAVIS

President, YM360

AARON AMMON

Project Manager

ANGELA TERRY

Director of Events

A 3-PART DEVOTIONAL EXPERIENCE
DESIGNED TO HELP YOU BECOME A DISCIPLE OF CHRIST.
IN A WORD, TO KNOW GOD AND MAKE HIM KNOWN.

The *New/Next/Now* Discipleship Bundle provides three powerful devotional experiences to help you grow from a new believer to an authentic disciple of Christ.

NEW: FIRST STEPS FOR NEW CHRIST-FOLLOWERS

One of the most used new believer resources in youth ministry, this powerful 4-week devotional experience will help new believers get off to a strong start on their new journey with Christ.

NEXT: GROWING A FAITH THAT LASTS

4-week devotional will help you take ownership of your faith. NEXT will teach: Why it's important to own your faith, What life's purpose has to do with God's mission, How to build spiritual habits that last a lifetime, and How to use the influence you already have for Christ.

NOW: IMPACTING YOUR WORLD FOR CHRIST (RIGHT NOW!)

You have the amazing potential to impact your world for Christ, not just some time in the future ... but right NOW! Today. Your world is rich with opportunities to share the hopeful message of the Gospel, and to show people the amazing difference Christ can make in their lives. Now will help you make the most of these opportunities!

TO VIEW SAMPLES OF *NEW, NEXT & NOW* AND TO ORDER, GO TO YM360.COM/DEVOBUNDLE

WHAT KEEPS YOU FROM BEING ALL THAT GOD HAS CALLED YOU TO BE?

Whatever it is, you need to know this: there is a better way. God wants you to face your fears and lean-in to who He desires you to be. If you're ready, Facing Your Fears is a great place to start.

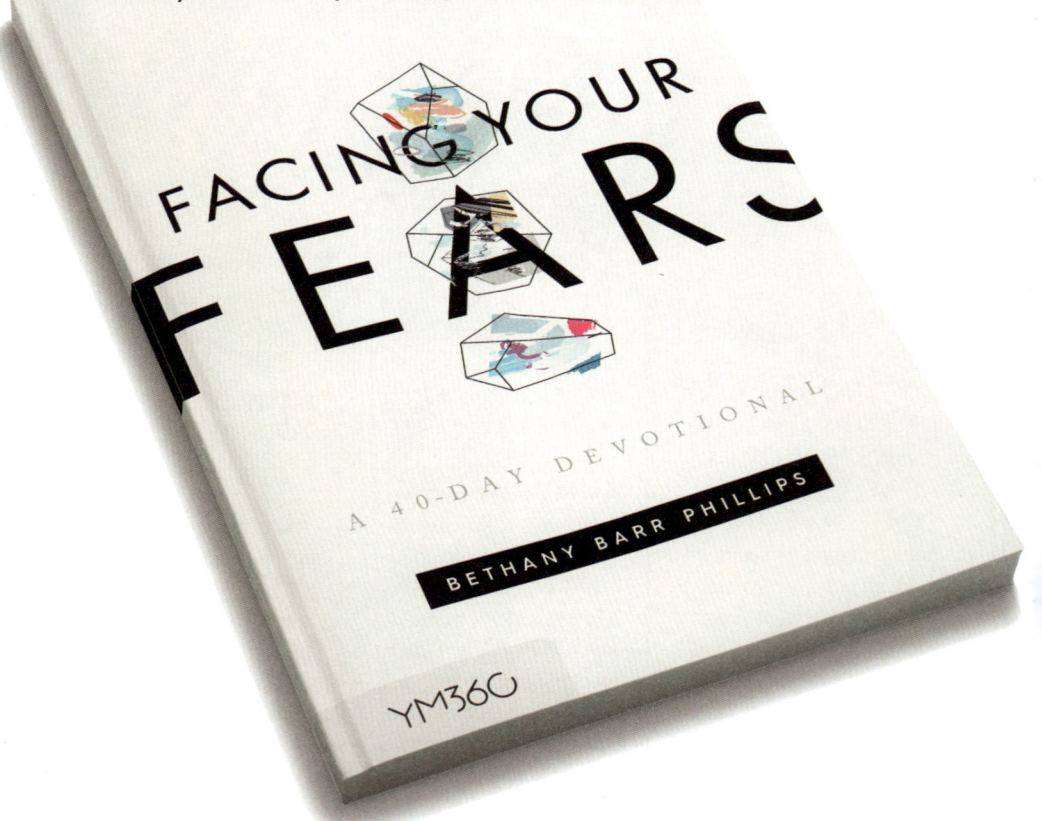

Facing Your Fears, a 40-day, Scripture-driven devotional by Bethany Barr Phillips, helps reveal where fear has taken hold of your life and equips you to put an end to these strongholds.

TO VIEW SAMPLES OF *FACING YOUR FEARS* & TO ORDER, GO TO YM360.COM/FEARS